POLAND IN WORLD WAR II

An Illustrated Military History

POLAND IN WORLD WAR II

An Illustrated Military History

ANDREW HEMPEL

HIPPOCRENE BOOKS, INC.
New York

FRONT COVER:
"To Arms" poster announcing the outbreak of the Polish Warsaw Uprising on August 1, 1944. The poster was designed and printed in the underground print shops of the Home Army prior to the uprising.

Paperback edition, 2005.
Copyright © 2000 Andrew Hempel

For information, address:
HIPPOCRENE BOOKS, INC.
171 Madison Avenue
New York, NY 10016

Library of Congress Cataloging-in-Publication Data

Hempel, Andrew.
    Poland in World War II : an illustrated military history /
  Andrew Hempel.
        p. cm.
    Includes bibliographical references and index.
    ISBN 0-7818-0758-1 hc
    ISBN 0-7818-1004-3 pb
        1. World War, 1939-1945--Poland. I. Title.

    D765 .H45 2000
    940.53'438--dc21

                                                    00-040677

Printed in the United States of America.

CONTENTS

HISTORICAL BACKGROUND

Poland entered into the family of European nations when Polish Prince Mieszko I and his court were baptized in 966. Mieszko's son, Boleslaw the Brave, was crowned the King of Poland in the Cathedral of Gniezno, the first Polish capital, in 1025.

A brief excursion into Polish history, with focus on a few milestones, will provide the historical background for the World War II events relating to Poland. In 1410 a combined Polish-Lithuanian army defeated the Order of Teutonic Knights in the Battle of Grunwald in northern Poland. At issue was an unceasing expansion of the Order in the easterly direction under the guise of so-called "conversion to Christianity" of the Lithuanians who had already been converted. This "conversion" was being administered with fire and sword.

In 1569 the Union of Poland and Lithuania was signed, a pact which was to last for over two hundred years. In 1572 the last king of the Jagiellonian dynasty died without leaving heirs to the throne, and thus the era of elected kings began, introducing a measure of democracy into the succession process. At that time, the Kingdom of Poland combined with the Grand Duchy of Lithuania was, except for the vast expanses of the Muscovy in the East, the largest state in Europe. It covered 900,000 square kilometers—nearly the size of New England, New York, Pennsylvania, Ohio, Michigan, Indiana, Kentucky, Virginia and West Virginia put together.

In the middle of the seventeenth century Poland was attacked by Turks, Tatars, Cossacks, Russians and Swedes and engaged in a series of wars which combined are referred to as the "Deluge." Eventually, Poland repulsed the aggressors, but the country was devastated and lay in ruins, never again to

1

return to its earlier wealth and power. This, in fact, marked the beginning of the end of the Kingdom of Poland. Still, the vestiges of greatness remained. In 1683, when the Turkish Grand Army besieged Vienna, Polish King John III Sobieski, responding to pleas from European states and from the Pope to save Austria and the rest of Europe from the onslaught of the heathens, mustered a European coalition which came to the rescue of the besieged city. In the ensuing battle, a powerful charge delivered by the heavy Polish cavalry, Husaria, destroyed the Turkish Army and freed Vienna.

Not quite a century later dismemberment (known as partitions of Poland) was begun by Poland's three neighbors: Russia, Prussia and Austria. In three successive territory seizures in 1772, 1793 and 1795, the three neighbors erased Poland from the maps of Europe. In 1791 Poland adopted the first democratic constitution in Europe and the second one in the world (after the United States), but it was already too late. Governed by absolute monarchs who were afraid to lose their monopoly of power, Russia with Prussia and Austria declared the constitution null and void. The Poles, among them Tadeusz Kosciuszko who participated also in the American Revolution, fought the invaders but lost against overwhelming odds. The French Revolution and the emergence of Napoleon Bonaparte gave the Polish patriots renewed hope: Napoleon, after all, had fought against all three partitioning powers. Polish Legions were formed and fought in all campaigns of the Napoleonic Army. (Poland's national anthem originates from these times.) However, after the final defeat of Napoleon at Waterloo in 1815, the Congress of Vienna drew European borders without an independent Poland, and thus crushed again Polish hopes for autonomy. Two Polish uprisings against Russia in 1830 and 1863 ended in

Polish Hussar. Over 3,000 knights, by charging against the Turkish Grand Army besieging Vienna in 1683, routed the enemy and freed the city.

defeat after much bloodshed. Thousands of the insurgents who survived were expropriated and deported to Siberia.

The First World War provided a realistic chance for Poland to restore its independence. The powers which had partitioned the country more than one hundred years earlier were fighting on opposite sides: Germany with the Austro-Hungarian Empire (the Central Powers) fought Imperial Russia allied with France and Great Britain. Polish troops, under their own banners, also joined the fight. At first, under the command of the anti-Russian revolutionary Józef Piłsudski, Polish legions were formed to fight Russia. But in 1917, after a number of successful operations against Russians, the legions were disbanded and Piłsudski was thrown into prison when the Poles refused to take an oath of allegiance to the Central Powers. Meanwhile, with the fall of its monarchy, Russia's grip on Poland loosened. This enabled the Poles to organize a Polish army in France to fight against the Central Powers. Russia was defeated first and Germany and Austria soon followed. Finally, on November 11, 1918, Poland re-emerged as a free nation after 123 years of captivity.

However, some problems remained. After the Communist Revolution Russia was determined to carry the flame, so successfully kindled at home, to Poland, Germany and beyond. In 1920, not quite two years after regaining independence, Poland was forced to fight again to maintain its sovereignty and to defend Europe. General Mikhail Tukhachevsky commanded the Soviet army. His Order of the Day, issued in Smolensk on July 2, 1920, read as follows:

> 'Soldiers of the Red Army!
> The time of reckoning has come!

The army of the Red Banner and the army of the preda-
tory White Eagle face each other in mortal combat!

Over the dead body of White Poland shines the road to
worldwide conflagration!

On our bayonets we shall bring happiness and peace to
toiling humanity!

To the West!

The hour of attack has struck!

On to Vilna, Minsk and Warsaw! March!'

Signed: commander in chief of the Western Front,
Tukhachevsky.

The Soviet army managed to occupy the eastern half of
Poland while the Poles fought a rearguard action. Some Soviet
units had already crossed the Vistula River, but on August 15,
1920, after a bloody five-day battle—described by Lord Edgar
Vincent d'Abernon as the "18TH decisive battle in world history"
and in Poland as the "Miracle on the Vistula"—the Soviet army
was stopped, repulsed and defeated. Remnants of the army
escaped to Russia in a complete rout. Those not taken prisoner
by the Poles crossed the Polish-German border only to be
interned by the Germans.

The brief, nineteen-year period of peace following the war
and lasting until 1939 was marked by a consolidation of the
three partitioned territories, which for over one hundred years
had belonged to different countries. Also, it marked a time of
vigorous economic growth for Poland. In the early 1920s
German intrigues in the Free City of Gdańsk prevented the free
flow of Polish trade through that port. Poland's response was to
build a new port in the small fishing village of Gdynia. By
1938, Gdynia became the busiest port in the Baltic Sea and

provided serious competition for Gdańsk. Also, in south-central Poland, construction of an industrial complex began in 1936. It consisted of hydroelectric power plants, steel works, aircraft manufacturing, machinery, ammunition and fertilizers. In 1938 Poland was the eighth largest producer of steel in the world. By the following year the population of Poland had reached 34.8 million.

In foreign policy, Poland had to perform a balancing act between Germany and Soviet Russia. In 1932 Poland signed a non-aggression pact with the Soviet Union, which was to last until 1945. In 1934 a similar ten-year pact was signed with Germany. One year earlier, shortly after Adolf Hitler's ascension to power, Polish Head of State Marshal Piłsudski made a secret proposal to France to mount together a preemptive strike against Germany to unseat Hitler before the Germans had time to rearm. But France refused, compelling the Poles to do the next best thing: to enter into a non-aggression pact with the Germans. In 1936 the Germans defied the Versailles treaty by reoccupying the demilitarized zone in the Rhineland, thus demonstrating to the world their aggressive intentions. As we now know, both non-aggression pacts were eventually broken by Hitler and Joseph Stalin.

After annexing Austria, Sudetenland and Czechoslovakia in March 1939, the German government repeated their request to Poland, demanding that Gdańsk become part of the Third Reich and that an extraterritorial highway and railroad be constructed across the so-called "Polish Corridor." The request was rejected by Poland—the first "No" Hitler encountered since coming to power in Germany. In April 1939 a mutual assistance treaty was concluded between Poland, France and Great Britain. On August 23, 1939, the Ribbentrop-Molotow pact was signed in

Moscow. In a secret protocol of the pact, plans for the fourth partition of Poland were drawn up by Hitler and Stalin, and the scene was set for the outbreak of World War II.

DEFENSE OF POLAND: SEPTEMBER 1 – OCTOBER 6, 1939

On September 1 at 4:45 A.M., fifteen-inch guns of the German battleship *Schleswig Holstein*, ostensibly paying a "good will visit to Gdańsk," opened fire on a 182-man garrison of the Polish fort Westerplatte. One hour later German forces crossed the 1,500-mile Polish-German frontier, attacking from the north, west and south. At the same time, massed German bombers flew in to attack Polish airfields, communication centers, troop concentrations and non-combatant civilians.

Below, a numerical comparison of Polish and German forces clearly shows German manpower and weapons superiority:

	Infantry (battalions)	Artillery (field guns)	Artillery (anti-tank guns)	Tanks	Aircraft
Poland	376	2,065	774	475	388
Germany	559	5,805	4,019	2,511	1,540 with 783 in reserve

With few exceptions, weapons deployed by the Polish army were not as modern as those used by the Germans. One notable exception was the Polish bomber *Łoś*, which was designed and built in Poland. At the time, it was one of the best planes of its type in Europe; but, production had just begun and Poland had only forty such machines. Polish fighter planes P-11 were

German and Soviet attack on Poland in 1939. Polish fighter P-11 used against German Luftwaffe, *and Polish crews of the modern* Łoś *bombers (visible in the background).*

German and Soviet attack on Poland in 1939. Polish infantry, cavalry, anti-tank and heavy artillery.

obsolete compared with the German *Messershmitts*. The German planes were often twice as fast, four to eight times better armed and able to fly higher than the Polish machines, but the Polish planes were more maneuverable. Polish pilots were superbly trained and by clever maneuvering were able to score victories— perhaps that is why German pilots called Polish planes "Wasps." Similarly, Polish pilots called their own planes "Bees."

On September 1, Germans bombed the main Polish airfields, but damage was relatively small; this is because, as early as August 27, all Polish military aircraft had been dispersed to small, well-camouflaged airfields scattered around Warsaw. Polish planes, although slow, were capable of taking off from and landing on small, improvised airfields. Under these circumstances, successes of Polish air force in air combat were as surprising as they were numerous. For example, between September 1–6, the Warsaw Fighter Brigade downed forty-three German aircraft and badly damaged another twenty-nine at a cost of thirty-eight own planes lost. Polish losses, although smaller in comparison with enemy losses, would have been unsustainable over any longer period of time. Poland did not have enough planes and pilots to endure over a long haul at that rate of attrition. Therefore, almost from the first day of the war, the German air force had complete mastery over Poland's skies.

Polish bomber aircraft attacked German columns very effectively, but often their losses were disproportionate to the inflicted damage. For example, on September 4, in only one day, the Poles lost nine *Łoś* bombers—one-fourth of what they had altogether.

From the very beginning, the Germans met with fierce resistance on the ground. The morale of the Polish army was very high, as the men knew that they were defending their country against a brutal aggressor and that their cause was ethically right. This conviction compensated in some measure for German advantage in number and quality of weaponry. Generally, Poles were much better at fighting at night, in close quarters, and in hand-to-hand encounters using bayonets. Germans had a greater advantage in the deployment of massed tanks and in the use of their air force for bombing raids—especially dive bombers and fighters used to strafe both Polish troop columns and civilians fleeing the Germans. The widespread notion that the Polish cavalry engaged in foolhardy attempts to charge German tanks in September 1939 is misleading. There were few isolated cases where Polish cavalrymen tried to break out between the tanks rather than surrender; but, as a rule, cavalrymen dismounted and operated like infantry before each engagement. Horses were used for transportation and were kept behind battle lines during an engagement. Each cavalry regiment was equipped with its own anti-tank and anti-aircraft artillery. Polish cavalry and infantry units were weaker in fire power and mobility than German panzer units, but their morale and determination helped enormously.

The initial struggle with the invader on September 1 is depicted in the personal account of a Polish officer who took part in the engagement. The battle was fought near the Polish-German border in southwest Poland where the Polish Wolhynian Cavalry Brigade was fighting against the attacking 4TH German Panzer Division:

> About 8:00 A.M. German tanks start the attack. Brigade units open fire from a very short distance, using their anti-tank artillery and anti-tank rifles. Surprised Germans withdraw, leaving behind a few destroyed tanks.

At 10:00 A.M. the Germans start a fifteen-minute artillery barrage. The defenders had not yet fully recovered when fifty to sixty tanks appear from the direction of Wilkowieck. They are coming in waves, but slowly and deliberately, remembering the earlier experience. They approach closer and closer, firing on the positions of the dug-in cavalrymen. The cavalrymen of the 4TH squadron wait until the tanks are five hundred yards or closer and then open murderous fire using their anti-tank rifles, artillery and heavy machine guns. Some tanks are set ablaze, spewing black smoke which reduces visibility to zero for the following waves of tanks. The tanks which follow avoid the burning and exploding wrecks only with great difficulties. With the last supreme effort, some tanks break through the Polish line and roll into the meadow crushing into the ground the anti-tank guns and their crews. Lieutenant Kantor's squadron is cut in half by the tanks which enter the meadow. He regroups both his wings so that one wing backs into the forest and the other is hidden in the orchards of the village Mokra. From there he continues to fire at the German tanks passing in front. The Germans lose their sense of direction and do not know where the fire comes from. With the help of Polish armored train summoned by Brigade Commander Colonel Filipowicz to support the 2ND Regiment of Horse Artillery, the attack is repulsed.

The next attack was mounted at 1:00 P.M. by over fifty tanks and infantry. The first defense line of the Polish Brigade could not repulse it, and thus the German tanks broke deep into the brigade positions nearly reaching the guns of the 2ND Regiment of Horse Artillery. In the duel between tanks and artillery, the tanks were gaining the upper hand. Colonel Filipowicz directed a counterattack of his reserves, which again, with the help of the armored train, repulsed the attackers. Returning to the narrative:

> The next attack at 3:00 P.M. is preceded by an attack of dive bombers. The Germans are initially successful. They direct their efforts to reach a road underpass below a rail viaduct, which would create an opening for the 4TH Panzer Division to the east. Polish soldiers are positioned on the railroad, in the forest and in the village Mokra. There are more and more tanks on the meadow. The focus of the attack is the viaduct. Several officers and many cavalrymen are killed. In the fierce battle, well-trained Polish soldiers do not surrender in the face of enemy superiority. Private Jan Kawiak, the anti-tank gun layer, demonstrates this to the fullest. On his own initiative, he chooses a favorable position for his gun about fifty yards from the viaduct. Firing from there, he destroys several enemy tanks. To keep him well-supplied with ammunition, other cavalrymen and even officers drag ammunition boxes to him ignoring enemy fire. On the battlefield, Lieutenant Colonel Kuczek nominates Private Jan Kawiak to Private 1ST Class. Under stronger and more effective Polish fire, there is confusion among the German tanks. The damaged tanks form fortress-like groups spitting fire in all directions. The others try to find a way out of the trap. Without reaching their objective, remnants of the armored group withdraw chaotically westward.

In their Polish campaign, the Germans applied a new tactic that came to be known as *Blitzkrieg*: by concentrating their armor, superior fire power of their artillery and air attacks, they were successful in breaching Polish lines. Exploiting these breakthroughs they thrust armored columns, penetrating the rear of Polish defenses. This tactic was facilitated by motorized transport, which proved much faster than the speed of Polish infantry and cavalry. Also, the strafing and bombing refugees increased chaos and terror, and blocked roads along which Polish troops were withdrawing.

On September 9, between Łódź and Warsaw, on the Bzura River, the Poles launched a counterattack which completely surprised the Germans: "What happened was really unbelievable," recollects German General Erich von Manstein. "Everything was going so well and according to plan, that it was difficult to imagine anything happening to change our plans." Yet, in reality, five Polish infantry divisions and four brigades of cavalry launched a surprise counterattack. When German command received news of Polish cavalry presence at the rear and flanks of their 30TH Infantry Division, they realized the severity of the situation. On September 11, they brought in reserves, but so did the Poles. After three days of bitter fighting, German materiel and manpower superiority finally tipped the scale, and German troops resumed their offensive.

On September 17, implementing the secret protocol of the Ribbentrop-Molotow pact, Soviet troops crossed the Polish-Soviet border. They encountered less resistance than the Germans, since an overwhelming majority of Polish troops had moved west to fight the Germans. This attack predetermined the hopelessness of the struggle against two powerful enemies attacking from the west and east. Poland did not surrender to

German and Soviet attack on Poland in 1939. Polish cavalry on the move during the battle on the Bzura River (notice the anti-tank artillery).

German and Soviet attack on Poland in 1939. A German plane shot down by the Poles.

the Germans or Russians, although further fighting was now hopeless. Henceforth, the Polish army fought only for its honor. The Germans had to pay dearly for every step eastward, and heavy fighting continued in central and eastern Poland. Four nests of resistance deserve honorable mention:

1.) Westerplatte. A Polish garrison of 182 near Gdańsk, Westerplatte was bombarded by the German battleship *Schleswig Holstein* since the first day of the war and was attacked continuously thereafter by German infantry. According to a pre-war plan, the garrison located in five bunkers was expected to hold out for six hours when attacked, by which time a relief column was supposed to reach the defenders. But, in actuality, no relief column ever arrived, and the garrison held out until food and ammunition were exhausted—that is, after seven days of fighting.

2.) Hel Peninsula. Located not far from Westerplatte, Hel Peninsula was attacked by air and by a barrage of artillery fire from two German battleships, *Schleswig Holstein* and *Schlesien*, on September 23. Under bombardment from land, air and sea, and under repeated attacks of German infantry, Polish defenders slowly withdrew along the peninsula. The garrison, after destroying weapons and equipment, laid arms on October 1 when stocks of ammunition, food and medical supplies were exhausted, and after hearing news that Warsaw had fallen.

3.) Defense of Warsaw. On September 8, units of the 1ST and 4TH German panzer divisions, together with the 31ST Infantry Division, reached Warsaw suburbs and attempted to seize the city. But they were met by heavy artillery and machine gun fire and were forced to withdraw. In the days that followed, repeated German attacks were also repulsed. On September 22, the German ring surrounding Warsaw was finally closed, cutting off access to the capital. Besides civilians, there were about ninety thousand Polish troops who had retreated to the city from the west and north. These troops had not been demoralized by earlier defeats and were ready to defend Warsaw to the end. In order to complete the Polish campaign, Hitler wanted to take Warsaw early, and to transfer his troops west to face the French and the British at his unprotected western border. From September 22–25, the city was subjected to a fierce artillery barrage and bombardment from the air. Polish anti-aircraft artillery managed to shoot down fifteen German planes. On September 26, the Germans began attacking along the perimeter of the defense but without success. Meanwhile, shortages of ammunition (each artillery piece had less than twenty rounds of ammunition left) and food, along with the threat of epidemic diseases caused by lack of water and a large number of human and animal corpses (which could not be buried fast enough), compelled the Polish commander of Warsaw to capitulate. A capitulation document was signed on September 28, and German troops entered the city on October 1. One day before the capitulation was signed, an emissary from Polish commander in chief Marshal Edward Śmigły-Rydz had arrived by plane to the besieged city with instructions to form an underground military organization. On September 28, just before the Germans entered Warsaw, the first meeting of the clandestine military organization was held in the Warsaw town hall.

4.) Southeastern Poland. The last battle of the 1939 campaign took place in southeastern Poland and was fought by the Polish Operational Group "Polesie" under the command of General Franciszek Kleeberg. On the evening of September 28, Polish cavalry units attacked the Soviet troops. The ensuing two-day battle was fought on the Soviet side with tanks, artillery and air force. Even though German units joined the fight, the

Polish Operational Group emerged from the battle undefeated. The Soviets then withdrew east beyond the demarcation line agreed upon with the Germans. A five-day battle against the Germans followed. The group was still undefeated, but now was without ammunition and supplies. General Kleeberg concluded that under these conditions further struggle against both aggressors would only put lives at stake without any prospect of success. He capitulated on October 6. His last order of the day to his troops ended with the words of the Polish national anthem: "Poland will not perish as long as we are alive." Elsewhere in Poland, but with the same words, cavalrymen of the 110TH Regiment of the Cavalry Brigade "Wolkowysk," commanded by Major Henryk Dobrzański-Hubal, attacked a German unit at Chodkowo village in the Kozienice Forest. Thus began partisan warfare against the invader.

German and Soviet attack on Poland in 1939. Soviet armored car destroyed in a battle with Polish troops.

The Polish navy consisted of five destroyers, five submarines, six minesweepers and a number of support vessels. Four days before the German attack, three destroyers were sent to England to carry on the struggle against Germany together with the British fleet. The ships which remained in the Baltic were, from the first day of the war, under constant attack from the German air force and suffered damage. Three submarines were interned in Sweden, and two managed to reach British shores. One of these, *Orzeł* (Eagle), was initially interned in Tallin, Estonia, where it arrived to disembark its commander who had contracted typhoid. Under German pressure, Estonians commandeered the submarine, seizing all maps and some armaments and torpedoes. On September 18, Polish sailors managed to disable electric installation in the port and under the cover of darkness guided the submarine out of the harbor despite Estonian artillery fire. The Poles reached British shores by using maps drawn from memory.

From then on, the Polish navy—fighting alongside its British allies, and later with the American navy in foreign seas—began a new chapter in its fight against Germany. Polish ships participated in the convoy services and in the 1944 Normandy landing. Also, the Polish destroyer *Piorun* fought in the battle against the German battleship *Bismarck*. For nearly an hour, in complete darkness, *Piorun* kept on a parallel course with the battleship, exchanging fire and signalling *Bismarck*'s position to the British fleet so that it could not escape. During this time, it would have only taken one artillery hit from the bigger German battleship (25-times its size) to sink the Polish destroyer within seconds. *Piorun*'s salvo weighed 290 pounds, whereas *Bismarck* was firing salvos weighing eight tons each.

German and Soviet attack on Poland in 1939. Polish submarine Orzeł and its commander, Captain J. Grudzinski; the submarine escaped internment in Tallin, Estonia, and without maps reached British shores.

Polish navy operating with the British fleet. Polish destroyer Piorun, which alone engaged the German battleship Bismarck in an hour-long artillery duel.

In the field of intelligence, the Poles provided the Allies with a priceless weapon: the ability to read the most secret German radio signals. Before the war, Polish cryptoanalysts had broken the secret of the German coding machine "Enigma" and had passed the secret, together with the reconstructed copy of the coding machine, to the French and the British two weeks before the outbreak of the war. The British made full use of that information, building a secret cryptological center at Bletchley Park, midway between Oxford and Cambridge. Throughout the war, they read German messages encoded on Enigma.

Polish war effort in the West. German coding machine "Enigma" and the three Polish cryptologists, M. Rejewski, H. Zygalski, and J. Różycki who, before the war, succeeded in building an exact copy of the German machine and breaking the German code.

But what happened to the French and British allies of Poland in September 1939? In accordance with the military discussions held with the French and the British in the summer of 1939, the Polish army was expected to engage the Germans for the two weeks required to launch a major offensive with seventy battle-ready French divisions across the Rhine. The Poles fulfilled their obligation, but the French and the British did not. The only "help" from these two allies was their declaration of war on Germany by September 3, three days after the Germans attacked Poland. However, these declarations were not followed by any hostile acts towards Germany. While the Polish army fought alone, ninety-two French divisions stood idle behind the Maginot Line facing thirty-five third-grade German divisions. Hitler's gamble that France and Britain would not attack ultimately paid off: he was able to use all his forces against Poland.

German losses in the Polish Campaign were as follows:

- 50,000 personnel, dead and wounded
- 1,000 tanks and armored cars (30 percent of what the Germans possessed at that time)
- 370 artillery pieces
- 600 planes (approximately 25 percent of what the *Luftwaffe* had in its arsenal)

In September 1939, in the war against the Germans, the Polish army suffered the following manpower losses: 66,300 killed, 133,700 wounded, and 420,000 taken prisoner. Most equipment and armaments of the Polish army were captured by the Germans. The Soviet army took 190,000 prisoners by the time hostilities from Polish regular army units ceased.

CONTINUED STRUGGLE FOR POLAND ABROAD

Following the defeat of Poland, officers and soldiers of the Polish army, air force and navy were either 1) captured by the Germans and sent to prisoner of war (POW) camps in Germany, or 2) were captured by the Soviets who imprisoned the officers in POW camps while the soldiers and non-commissioned officers were distributed throughout the vast Soviet Gulag system. Many officers and soldiers managed to escape into Romania, Hungary and Lithuania where they were interned. Since these countries were neutral and friendly to Poland, particularly Romania and Hungary, it was not impossible to avoid internment. With the help of Polish embassies and consulates in these countries, thousands obtained passports and then traveled via Yugoslavia and Italy (not yet at war against the Allies) to France. There were also some officers and soldiers who managed to discard Polish military uniforms and succeeded in avoiding capture by either the Germans or the Soviets. Many later joined the underground movement. Finally, there were those like Captain Dobrzański-Hubal mentioned earlier who did not accept defeat; in small groups, they carried on armed resistance against the Germans, still wearing their Polish military uniforms.

Poland, as a state, never surrendered to the Germans or Russians. Indeed, on September 30, 1939, in accordance with the Polish Constitution, Polish President Ignacy Mościcki, who was interned in Romania, resigned and nominated Władysław Raczkiewicz (who at that time was in Paris) to the post of Polish president. At the same time, the Polish government also interned in Romania resigned. This permitted the new Polish president to entrust the formation of a new government to General Władysław

Sikorski who was in France at the time. A new government was formed with General Sikorski as prime minister and commander in chief, thus maintaining continuity of the Polish State and Polish participation in the war. The Government in Exile, which moved to England after the fall of France, functioned in London throughout the war and beyond. When it lost accreditation in England, France, the United States and in other countries— which recognized instead the communist puppet regime imposed on Poland by the Soviets after the war—the Government in Exile continued its struggle against communism until 1990, when the Soviet Union disintegrated and Poland regained its freedom. In the same year, fifty years after the formation of the Polish Government in Exile, a ceremony was held in the rebuilt Royal Palace in Warsaw and President in Exile Kaczorowski handed over the Polish State insignia to Lech Wałęsa, the democratically elected president of Poland; the insignia had been kept by the Polish Government in Exile in London while Poland was under foreign occupations by the Germans and Soviets.

NARVIK

The new Polish government in France immediately began to form Polish armed forces on French soil. Those who escaped to France from Poland—volunteers from Polish communities in France, Britain and throughout the world—provided manpower for the organized formations. On April 8, 1940, the Germans attacked Denmark and Norway. On May 8, the Polish Podhalanska (mountain) Brigade, together with the British 24TH Guards Brigade, two French battalions and one Norwegian battalion, landed on the Norwegian island of Hinnoy and prepared to attack Narvik, which had already been occupied by the Germans. Although Narvik was taken by the expeditionary forces on May 29, an order was received on June 3 for the allies to evacuate to France and then to England. The Polish brigade lost one hundred men killed in the fighting. Also, the Polish submarine *Orzeł* was lost in Norwegian waters with six officers and forty-nine seamen aboard.

DEFENSE OF FRANCE

The Polish forces in France, just prior to the German attack, consisted of the ready-for-combat First Grenadier Division and Second Infantry Fusiliers Division. One armored cavalry brigade and two infantry divisions were in the process of formation. Also, the Polish Independent Carpathian Brigade was formed in Syria (a French protectorate at that time), where many Polish soldiers had fled from Romania. The Polish air force in France consisted of eighty-six aircraft in four squadrons. One and a half squadrons were fully operational, and the rest were in various stages of training.

On May 10, 1940, Hitler launched his attack against France, Belgium and Holland. He attacked with 114 infantry divisions, 10 panzer divisions, 6 motorized divisions, 1 cavalry division and 1 airborne division—in all, with 2,700 tanks and 3,800 aircraft. Against those forces, the Western Allies manned the Maginot Line and in addition deployed 122 infantry divisions, 3 infantry brigades, 3 armored divisions, 3 light tank divisions—in all, with 3,200 tanks, 400 armored cars and 1,924 aircraft. It is evident that the German forces did not have an overwhelming materiel superiority over the Allies. What they did have, however, was the *Blitzkrieg* strategy which they had used for the first time in Poland seven months earlier. This demonstrably successful German strategy had been ignored by the general staffs of the Western Allies, who superficially dismissed Poland's defeat as clearly unavoidable. In actuality, French, British, Dutch and Belgian resistance against the German attack lasted thirty-nine days, from May 10 until June 18, when General Henri Petain asked the Germans for an armistice. At Compiegne, on June 22, France capitulated to Hitler. Seven months earlier, Poland had fought alone against the Germans and, since September 17, against the Soviets. The struggle lasted thirty-six days, from September 1 until October 6, when General Kleeberg's group laid down their arms in eastern Poland. German sources report that in the 1939 campaign against Poland, they used 400 million rifle bullets, 2 million artillery shells and 70,000 aerial bombs. In their campaign against France in 1940, the Germans used less than half of that amount to induce France to capitulate.

In 1940 the First Polish Grenadier Division was deployed southwest of Nancy, France, where in a two-day battle at Lagarde on June 17 and 18 it defended successfully its sector but had to withdraw because retreating French divisions exposed both of its flanks to the enemy. On June 18, Marshal Petain approached the Germans for an armistice. On June 19, a radio bulletin from General Sikorski announced that Poland would continue to fight as an ally of Great Britain. Sikorski ordered the Polish units to reach the French ports in the north, west and south—or if that would prove impossible, to cross the Swiss frontier. The Second Infantry Fusiliers Division was deployed in the vicinity of Belfort, near the Swiss frontier. The

27

Defense of France in 1940. Polish 10TH Armored Cavalry Brigade smashing a battalion from the German 66TH Motorized Regiment.

division stopped the advancing Germans in a two-day battle on the hills of Clos-du-Doubs; but again, in view of the ongoing French-German armistice talks and General Sikorski's order, the division crossed the Swiss frontier in the evening of June 19. From June 13–16, the 10TH Armored Cavalry Brigade, still being formed, fought in the area of Champaubert and Montbard, approximately sixty miles northwest of Dijon. On the night of June 16, realizing the futility of continuing the battle, the brigade destroyed its equipment and moved south in small groups to reach Atlantic ports and escape to England.

Defense of France in 1940. Ready for action: Polish Moran fighter planes on a French airfield.

After the French surrendered, the Polish Carpathian Brigade in Syria moved to the British Protectorate of Palestine to continue the fight against the Germans alongside the British. In August 1941, the Brigade was moved to Tobruk where, together with the Australians and the British, they successfully defended the fortress until January 1942 when they were relieved by the British Eighth Army. From there, the brigade was withdrawn to Egypt and then to Palestine for reorganization into a division. The Polish air force in France, with its eighty-six fighter planes, shot down fifty German aircraft during the campaign, losing eleven of its own pilots in the air and fifteen on the ground. Most of the pilots and ground crews, despite opposition from French authorities, managed to escape to England by air directly from France or by sea through North Africa.

THE POLISH AIR FORCE IN GREAT BRITAIN

Having conquered France, Hitler now focused his attention on Great Britain. The planned invasion of the British Isles was given the code name "Sea Lion." The German fleet commander Grand Admiral Raeder laid down an essential condition for success of the operation: the absolute superiority of the German air force. Marshal Herman Goering, commander of the German air force, was quite confident that he could chase the British out of the skies. He had at his disposal 2,800 aircraft, of which 1,400 were medium-range bombers, 300 were dive bombers, 800 were single-seat fighters (*Messerschmitt* 109) and 300 were two-seat fighters (*Messerschmitt* 110). Against this Armada, Great Britain could only muster 57 squadrons with 531 Spitfires and Hurricanes.

The Fighter Command was headed by 60-year-old air chief Marshal Sir Hugh Dowding, who would not have had much chance of winning the battle against such odds had he not possessed a great advantage, shrouded in utmost secrecy: the ability to read the most secret German radio signals, using the replica of the German coding machine "Enigma." As mentioned earlier, these codes were passed on to the British by Polish Intelligence before the war. Marshal Dowding belonged to the very small group of people who knew the Enigma secret. Since he was able to read Goering's messages, he knew his intentions and could deploy his squadrons in the most efficient manner, often incomprehensive to those who did not know the secret. In this way, he was able to compensate for the enemy's superiority in numbers.

Approximately 1,500 Royal Air Force pilots took part in the Battle of Britain, over 150 of whom were Polish. This was the largest contingent of foreign pilots fighting with the British against the Germans. Half of the Poles flew in British squadrons, and the other half in the two Polish squadrons, 302 and 303. The 302 squadron became operational on August 15; the 303 squadron followed suit on August 30, albeit in a most irregular fashion when Lieutenant Paszkiewicz shot down a German Dornier bomber without orders during a training flight. For this, he received concurrently a reprimand and a commendation. On August 2, squadron 303 was formed around the nucleus of the pilots from the old First Warsaw Air Regiment. These pilots had already bagged several kills in Poland and in France. During the Battle of Britain, squadron 303 became the highest scoring allied squadron. The Poles used their own tactics to achieve these results, and occasionally the British were skeptical as to whether the number of kills claimed by the Poles

Polish air force in Britain. Squadron 303 pilots returning from a successful mission during the Battle of Britain.

Polish air force in Britain. On September 26, 1940, during the Battle of Britain, Polish commander in chief General W. Sikorski and King George VI visited squadron 303 at their base in Northolt; on that day, the squadron scored 11 downs with no losses of their own.

was not exaggerated. One of the doubters was British Group Captain Vincent. On one occasion, when squadron 303 went into action, he took a plane and followed them. The squadron met a large enemy formation over the London docks. Two Hurricanes immediately climbed high above, while the rest hung back with Vincent behind them. Then, the two lone planes dived almost vertically onto the Germans, spitting fire and pretending to ram them. This forced the bombers to break formation. "The Poles behind," writes Vincent, "jumped on the scattered planes and suddenly the air was full of burning aircraft, parachutes and pieces of disintegrating wings. It was all so rapid that it was staggering." Vincent tried to join in himself, but each time he fixed on a German plane, it disintegrated before his eyes as a Pole got there first. "I returned to Northolt feeling old and musty," he writes, "and told Wilkins [the intelligence officer] that what they claimed, they did indeed get!"

The Polish successes were often ascribed by the British to "the almost incredible audacity" of the Poles. One example was the case of pilot Stanisław Skalski, who flew with the British squadron 501 during the Battle of Britain. Skalski, badly burnt the second time he was shot down, slipped out from the hospital where he was recovering and rejoined his squadron. He was left with such a terror of fire that he could not even bear to light a cigarette, but he did not admit this to his British commanding officer. He insisted upon going operational, even though his leg was so badly wounded that he could not run during a scramble and therefore had to sit in his plane for hours awaiting the signal. Eventually, he became an accomplished ace with twenty-two enemy planes destroyed, six in Poland in 1939 and sixteen in Great Britain. In 1943 he was the commander of the County of London British 601 squadron.

Polish air force in Britain. Wing Commander Skalski, Polish air force ace of the Second World War.

Polish air force in Britain. The Standard of the Polish air force in Britain was made secretly by Polish women in German-occupied Poland and smuggled across German-ruled Europe; here it is being passed from one squadron to another.

Polish air force in Britain. Exceptional flying skills were required to bring this bomber from the Ruhr back home.

Polish air force in Britain. Flight Sergeant H. Pietrzak (top left) after scoring 500TH kill of the Polish air force in Britain.

Polish air force in Britain. Mascots of the 316 Fighter squadron.

But, the Battle of Britain was really just the beginning, though a very momentous one. By the start of 1941 there was a full-fledged Polish air force operating alongside the Royal Air Force. With ten fighter and four bomber squadrons and supporting services, it was larger than the combined air forces of the Free French, Dutch, Belgians and all other European allies operating from Britain. The Polish air force not only played a crucial role in the Battle of Britain in 1940, it also contributed significantly to the allied war effort in the air. It destroyed 770 enemy aircraft, shot down 190 flying bombs aimed at London, dropped 13,206 tons of bombs, and laid 1,502 mines. It destroyed over 1,000 enemy tanks and took part in virtually every type of Royal Air Force operation—all this at a cost of 1,973 killed and 1,388 wounded.

JEWS UNDER GERMAN OCCUPATION— THE "FINAL SOLUTION"

The Holocaust of the Jewish population in Europe during the Second World War is widely known. Poland's population in 1939 was 34.8 million, of which 3.4 million were Jews. No other European country could even come close to the number of Jewish people living within its borders. The Germans, ever efficient and practical and having decided on the extermination of the Jews, earmarked Poland as a place to carry out their plan, as this would minimize transportation effort. In 1940 the first ghettos were established, among those the Warsaw Ghetto, where Jewish people were initially allowed to exist. Concentration camps were also set up by the Germans throughout Poland. Auschwitz, the largest of the camps, was initially used for Polish prisoners. On June 14, 1940, the first 728 Polish prisoners were brought to Auschwitz, and for the next twenty-one months the camp was inhabited almost exclusively by Poles. The first transport of fifteen hundred Jews arrived to Auschwitz on May 12, 1942. It is estimated that the victims of the Auschwitz-Birkenau concentration camp alone number approximately 1,500,000, of whom most were Jews and 150,000 were Christian Poles.

On April 19, 1943, when the Germans began the final liquidation of the Warsaw Ghetto, about six hundred Jewish fighters started an uprising which, with materiel help from the Polish underground Home Army, lasted until May 16, 1943. At this time, all of the Jews were murdered by the Germans, except for a few who escaped from the ghetto through sewers with the help of the underground Polish Home Army. German losses in the uprising were three hundred killed and one thousand wounded.

Poland was the only country in German-occupied Europe where hiding Jews was punishable by death. The penalty applied equally, and without regard to age or gender, to the hidden Jews and to all Christian members of the host family. Despite this, of all the European nations, Poland saved the greatest number of Jews. Indeed, on December 4, 1942, in cooperation with the Polish Government in Exile in London, Polish underground organizations in occupied Poland established the underground organization "Żegota" in Warsaw, exclusively dedicated to saving and helping the Jews. Żegota provided living quarters, false documents, food, medical care and financial help to the Jews in what was a difficult and dangerous operation. Many Hassidic Jews, especially in the provinces of eastern Poland, wore distinctive black attire which, in addition to their features, immediately betrayed their Semitic origin. Therefore, it was imperative that they stay indoors at all times, supplied with necessary provisions from Żegota members.

Many Jewish children were saved in monasteries and convents by religious order nuns. In these circumstances, the children were taught Christian prayers and were often baptized for security reasons, in case of German inspections, and in some cases because of the missionary zeal of the nuns. Many Jews and rabbis resented this and to this day often harbor anger for conversions of the children into Christianity. But overall, the greatest number of Jews saved in Poland during that time were saved by individual Polish families.

Jews under German occupation. Erection of a ten-foot wall around the Warsaw Ghetto.

Jews under German occupation. Fighters of the Jewish Combat Organization.

Jews under German occupation. Jews dragged out of the bunkers and led to execution.

Jews under German occupation. After being searched and robbed, the Jews were immediately shot.

Western leaders were informed about the plight of the Jews under the German occupation. The most complete information was transmitted by Jan Karski, a secret courier who traveled across German-conquered Europe between the Polish Underground Organization in Poland and the Polish Government in Exile in London. In October 1942, before his departure to London and at a considerable risk to his life, Karski was smuggled twice in and out of both the Warsaw Ghetto and the Belzec extermination camp in order to obtain firsthand information. Karski related what he had seen when he met with Polish, Jewish, British and American representatives in London and Washington, including President Franklin Delano Roosevelt. Requests from Jewish leaders to bomb Germany as retribution for the extermination of Jews came to naught.

GERMAN TERROR AND THE POLISH UNDERGROUND STATE

During the invasion of Poland in 1939, the Germans offered a foretaste of what was to come. They introduced and applied fully the notion of "total war," which treated civilians as military adversaries and in most cases blatantly violated the Geneva convention of military conduct. Violations included: indiscriminate air strafing of columns of refugees escaping eastward, shooting at Polish pilots coming down on parachutes, and even in some cases shooting prisoners of war. The German objective was to terrorize and subdue the Poles by all available means. This policy, refined, broadened and intensified, was continued when the military operations ceased and the occupation of Poland began. On August 22 and 23, 1939, one week before the German invasion of Poland,

Hitler, at a secret meeting with the senior commanders of the German forces in Obersalzberg, Germany, declared the following:

> Destruction of Poland is the first priority. Our most important objective is the total destruction of the living resources of Poland and not to reach a particular line drawn on a map. I shall give the ministry of propaganda some justification, true or not, for our attack on Poland. Nobody in the future will ask the victor if he was truthful or not. If one decides to start and conduct the war, legality does not matter, what matters is victory. Pity and compassion have to be eliminated from your thinking. You have to be brutal because the stronger is always right. Therefore, I have prepared and ordered my SD units [*Sicherheit Dienst*—skull and crossbones] to kill without mercy men, women and children of Polish origin.

The western and central parts of Poland annexed by the Germans (eastern Poland was occupied by the Soviets) were subdivided into two parts. The western and northern parts were incorporated into the German Reich, and the south-central part was named General Government (GG) and was administered by German Governor Hans Frank who resided in Wawel, the Royal Palace in Cracow.

The Poles did not have the right to live in the territories incorporated into the German Reich. Polish people were thrown out of their houses and apartments, allowed fifteen minutes to gather up to one hundred pounds of personal belongings, and were forced to leave behind businesses, estates and homes without any compensation. They all had to move to General Government. There was even a detailed German plan to destroy Polish culture and to annihilate Polish writers, scientists, and educated people. In the annexed territories and in the GG, all Polish schools of higher learning, high and middle schools, theaters, and museums were closed down. The playing of Fryderyk Chopin's music was forbidden (although Poles organized underground concerts). The Royal Palace in Warsaw was burnt to the ground in November 1939, when Warsaw was already occupied by the Germans. According to Heinrich Himmler's plan, Poles had to know only how to count to five hundred, how to sign their names, and to know enough German to understand German orders.

On November 6, 1939, 183 professors of the six centuries-old Jagiellonian University in Cracow were arrested and sent to Sachsenhausen concentration camp. Similar roundups occurred in other Polish cities and in institutions of higher learning. Poles were not allowed to have radios or automobiles. Those Poles who still lived in the annexed territories were forbidden to speak Polish on the streets and in public places. They were not allowed to travel without a German permit. In the cities of GG, the Germans organized roundups of Polish passersby by closing several city blocks, then catching and loading people onto trucks and sending them to concentration or labor camps.

There were frequent mass executions of Poles in forests, in public, and on city streets, particularly in Warsaw where a number of prisoners brought from the notorious Pawiak prison were shot in full view of rounded up passersby. After the executions, sidewalks where the shootings took place were covered with flowers brought by the people of Warsaw. Even today, throughout Warsaw, commemorative plaques on houses mark the spots where executions took place.

In this environment of unmitigated terror, in the area of the General Government, an unprecedented secret Underground

State was organized. At the head of the organization was a civilian, the Government in Exile's delegate. Twelve underground departments were set up, similar to the ministries and departments within the United States or any other democratic country. For example, the underground Department of Education and Culture coordinated underground high school courses. In 1944, two thousand high school courses operated in occupied Poland. In the same year ten thousand students attended underground universities throughout the GG area. Lectures, tutorials and exams were conducted in private apartments and with small groups of students. Teachers and professors moved from one group to another for two or three-hour sessions. These travels were connected with danger because of the aforementioned German roundups. The lack of laboratories and other accessories of higher education was amply compensated by the students' exceptional zeal and hunger for knowledge.

German occupation of Poland. Notorious Gestapo "Pawiak" prison in Warsaw. Prisoners shot in mass executions were kept there.

German occupation of Poland. Pacification of the Rzeszow Province. In a matter of minutes, the men pictured were dead.

German occupation of Poland. After the execution.

The Culture section of the department was engaged in preserving, securing, and hiding Polish art treasures from German plunder or destruction. One notable outcome of that program was the preservation and concealment of the famous 15 by 33-foot "Battle of Grunwald" painting. After the war had started, the painting was evacuated to Lublin where the rolled up canvas was hidden in a very long counter top in the local museum. Upon news that the Germans were going to requisition and move into the museum building, the rolled up canvas, weighing one and one-half tons, was smuggled out of the museum building during the night. The painting was hermetically packed, buried in a trench, and covered by a concrete slab in a municipal transportation shed near Lublin. The Germans were so anxious to confiscate the painting that they advertised a ten million marks reward for help in its capture. It is significant that despite a great number of people who were involved in the whole operation, or who knew about it, not one person betrayed the secret to the Germans. Although "black sheep" surfaced here and there, as in any other society, this episode reveals the moral principles and patriotism of the Polish people under German occupation. After the war, the painting was retrieved and underwent a thorough restoration process. It now hangs in the National Museum in Warsaw.

Returning to the Underground State, there was also an underground parliament consisting of seventeen representatives from eight political parties. The underground army was called Home Army (AK) to distinguish it from the Polish armed forces operating abroad. The Home Army, numbering four hundred thousand, was the largest underground army in German-occupied Europe. Its commander, General Grot, reported to the Government's delegate, thus preserving civilian control over the armed forces.

German occupation of Poland. The sign of fighting Poland. "P" stood for "Poland," "W" for "Walczy" ("Fights" in Polish). The "W" also signified an anchor—a symbol of hope. Signs such as these appeared around Warsaw and other Polish cities.

The role of the Home Army was to carry out the struggle against the German occupant. This involved training new soldiers and amassing equipment for the general uprising against the Germans when an opportune moment arrived. It also involved attacking and destroying the most vital and vulnerable infrastructure of the enemy's war effort and terror machine. Thus, in the countryside, partisan units blew up trains, liquidated Gestapo agents, launched attacks on prisons to free Polish political prisoners, and defended the local population against German excesses. For example, the Zamość region (southeastern Poland) was earmarked by the Germans for colonization by members of the SS (*Schutzstaffel*, Hitler's Nazi protection echelon) and their families. Polish farmers were ordered to leave their farms, and if their children had a blond, "Aryan" look, they were taken away from their parents and loaded on a train to Germany. But, that train stopped in Warsaw for the night, and Polish railway men spread the news of the children aboard to the Warsowians. By the next morning all of the children had been taken into the homes of Polish families in Warsaw. Eventually, the German colonization of the Zamość region ceased after several Polish attacks on the German-colonized villages.

An important action carried out by Home Army intelligence agents was the identification and location of German plants and experimental installations which were building and testing V-1 and V-2 rockets at Peenemunde on the island of Usedom on the Baltic Sea. Exact locations of the plants were transmitted to Warsaw and then to London by the Home Army. On August 18, 1943, using the transmitted information, British bombers destroyed the plants at Peenemunde so thoroughly that there was nothing left to repair or rebuild. The Germans were forced to start anew, this time in southeastern Poland. But, the Home Army discovered the new site and put it under observation. On May 20, 1944, they spotted a V-2 rocket which, without exploding, had landed on a marshy terrain. Local villagers who were in close contact with the Polish Home Army immediately hid the 45 by 5-foot rocket with reeds and bushes in order to confound German search parties. The rocket was then disassembled by Home Army engineers and flown to England on July 25, 1944, aboard a Dakota aircraft specially sent by the British. All this took place right under the noses of the Germans, who were stationed less than a mile away.

In the cities, particularly in Warsaw, the underground Home Army fought the Germans by selectively killing those SS and Gestapo officers known for their cruelty and brutality towards Polish prisoners; by virtue of their rank, these officers were responsible for the terror reigning in occupied Poland. One of the better known actions was the assassination, on February 1, 1944, of General Franz Kutschera, who was the chief of German police for the Warsaw district. Twelve Home Army participants, nine young officers and three young female intelligence agents took part in the attack. As in every action of this kind, the team consisted of the attack group, the cover group, the reconnaissance group (intelligence) and the automobile drivers. Three automobiles were employed in that particular action, one of which was to transport wounded participants. Medical teams were also waiting in predetermined parts of the city, and Home Army doctors stood by to take care of the wounded. Kutschera was stopped in his chauffeur-driven car by one of the Home Army automobiles just before reaching the SS headquarters building; he was killed together with his chauffeur at point-blank range. Two members of the attack group, already

German occupation of Poland. Soldiers of the underground Home Army 27ᵀᴴ Wolhynian Infantry Division.

German occupation of Poland. Colors detachment platoon of the 6ᵀᴴ company, 26ᵀᴴ Infantry Division of the Home Army.

under fire from the SS headquarters building, jumped into the general's car to search for his identification papers. (Obtaining identification papers was a standing order for operations of that kind.) By the time they found them, they were both wounded— despite covering fire from the cover team—and were taken in one of the cars to an underground clinic. They immediately underwent surgery, but died from their wounds two days later. Two other members of the team escaped in one of the cars but found themselves trapped on one of the Vistula bridges, blocked on both sides by the SS. The two attackers, after exhausting their ammunition, jumped into the river and were killed by Germans firing from the bridge. The rest of the group avoided capture. The whole action at the SS headquarters lasted for one minute and forty seconds. As a reprisal, the Germans shot one hundred prisoners from the Pawiak prison at the spot where Kutschera was assassinated; another two hundred were shot in the ghetto ruins near the prison itself. Before his death, Kutschera had planned to marry Himmler's sister. It is said that since the Germans refused to "recognize" the Polish assassination, the ceremony, in a macabre way, took place anyway: Himmler's sister marrying the cadaver.

Similarly executed actions on important German purveyors of terror resulted in high Polish casualties; for, in reprisals, the Germans killed great numbers of prisoner hostages. The German terror and Polish counter-terror meted out to the German perpetrators soon developed into a deadly contest of endurance and wills. In 1943 nine successful actions against the cruelest high-ranking Gestapo officers were carried out. In 1944 six similar assassination operations were successfully executed. During the course of these and other open battles, 361 Gestapo or SS functionaries in 1943, and 584 in 1944, were liquidated by the underground Polish Home Army in Warsaw alone. The Poles won the deadly contest, because after the assassination of Kutschera, the German terror markedly slackened.

The struggle was not confined to the use of firearms or explosives. There was a highly developed underground press, which was printed in underground printing shops. Some papers had a circulation as high as ten thousand. Apart from publications in Polish, underground printing shops also printed booklets and leaflets in impeccable German, purporting to come from secret anti-Hitler German organizations located in Germany. These booklets and leaflets exposed the hopelessness of continued struggle against the Allies (Action "N" carried out by the underground Information Department). Underground printing shops made posters in German with false information, including one such order in February 1944 calling for all Germans to evacuate GG, and another order to register all household cats.

German occupation of Poland. German sign warning German units about particularly active Polish guerilla operations in the area.

German occupation of Poland. General Grot-Rowecki, the military commander of the Polish Underground Home Army from 1940 until 1943. He was arrested in 1943 and murdered in early August of 1944 (in the first days of the Warsaw Uprising) in the Sachsenhausen concentration camp. After the arrest, General Bór-Komorowski took over the command.

German occupation of Poland. The fallen participants of the Kutschera assassination, and the Vistula bridge under which "Sokol" and "Juno" were shot.

German occupation of Poland. The survivors of the Kutschera assassination with the intelligence chief "Rayski" of the "Parasol" battalion.

As demonstrated by the above, humor could often be used as an effective weapon. The building of the Polish Academy of Science was used by the German Gendarmerie as barracks. German sentries were posted in front of the building, and a little further on stood the statue of Nicolaus Copernicus, the Polish astronomer. The Germans maintained of course that Copernicus was German, and so they removed the Polish plate from the pedestal, substituting it with a German one. But, on one winter morning in broad daylight, a small truck arrived with two young men who, in full view of the sentries, unscrewed the German plate, loaded it on the truck and departed. Within a few days, German posters appeared around Warsaw stating: "Criminal elements have removed German plate from the Copernicus statue. German authorities are removing therefore the monument of Kilinski from its pedestal." (Colonel Jan Kilinski, a cobbler and a Polish national hero, had led an uprising against the Russians in Warsaw in 1794.) Soon after, similar posters appeared around the city. The posters read: "Criminal elements have removed the statue of Kilinski, I order therefore one month extension of winter weather on the Eastern Front. Signed Nicolaus Copernicus." The Warsawians surely had a good laugh.

SOVIET OCCUPATION AND THE POLISH ARMY IN THE SOVIET UNION

Polish prisoners of war taken by the Russians in 1939 were divided into two groups: approximately 15,000 officers and policemen, who were sent to three camps—Kozielsk, Starobielsk and Ostaszkow; and 190,000 privates and non-commissioned officers, who were distributed throughout the vast Gulag system.

German occupation of Poland. Copernicus monument and the Polish Academy of Science building as it looks today. During the German occupation, it was used as Gendarmerie barracks. German sentries were posted under the arches.

Also, in an effort to destroy Polish presence in eastern Poland, which was annexed by the Soviets on the strength of the Ribbentrop-Molotow pact of 1939, entire Polish families were expropriated and deported in 1940 and 1941 from these territories to Siberia and Kazachstan. The deportees often belonged to the more educated class, or were those who owned houses and land. Commonly, men were arrested first and deported separately. Women and children were deported later and to a different part of the vast Gulag network, so that husbands and wives did not know where their spouses were exiled. Mortality, especially among children during the deportations and after, was extremely high.

On June 22, 1941, employing the *Blitzkrieg* strategy, Hitler attacked the Soviet Union and German armies moved deep into Soviet territory. Under pressure from victorious Germans and the British promising aid, on July 30, 1941, Stalin signed an agreement with the Polish Government in Exile in London. This agreement, among other provisions, stipulated mutual aid in the war against Hitler, "amnesty for Polish citizens deprived of freedom on the Soviet territory," and the formation of a Polish army under a commander appointed by the Polish Government in London. Polish General Władysław Anders, released from the NKVD (People's Commissariat of Internal Affairs) prison in Moscow, was nominated to that post. In response to the agreement, freed Polish Gulag prisoners began a trek across Russia to the assembly point of Buzuluk near Kuibyshev. Their journeys took weeks, even months to complete and involved spending nights on stations in hungry cities, waiting days at a time for erratically running trains. Many of these former prisoners, weakened by their Gulag existence, died from dysentery, typhus, exhaustion or starvation during their journeys or upon arrival. However, the number of officers arriving in Buzuluk was much smaller than expected. Stalin, when asked about this, replied that the officers had escaped to . . . Manchuria.

By the middle of March 1942, about seventy thousand Polish ex-prisoners of war assembled at Buzuluk. But the Poles received rations for only forty thousand, and the freed prisoners were dying fast, housed in tents in −50°F temperatures. Most importantly, they had received hardly any weapons from the Russians. Therefore, during negotiations with Stalin, General Anders succeeded in obtaining his agreement for the evacuation of the Polish army to Persia (now Iran), where they would be supplied and equipped by the British. The evacuation took place in two phases: one in April, and the other in August 1942. Altogether, about 113,000 people were evacuated, including women and children (mostly orphans). This was only a small fraction of the 1,500,000 Polish prisoners of war, deportees and Gulag inmates taken by the Soviets between 1939 and 1941. Most of them never saw Poland again.

After arrival in Persia, the army was moved to Iraq where it was equipped by the British and reorganized. After the French surrender in 1940, the Carpathian Brigade moved from Syria to Palestine, then defended Tobruk and joined the Polish army in Iraq to form the 2ND Polish Corps. The women and children, families of the military who came out of the Soviet hell, were transferred by the British to special camps in India and central Africa where they could recuperate. They had survived the war in safety.

On April 13, 1943, Berlin radio announced that in the village of Katyń, in the vicinity of Smolensk, Russia, the Germans had discovered mass graves of Polish officers. The Soviets announced that the Germans performed the killings in 1941 when invading the Soviet Union, and the Germans placed the

Polish army in the USSR. Following release from the Gulags, Polish prisoners came to the Polish recruiting center to join the forming Polish army. The photograph shows the arrival of recruits in Totskoye.

Polish army in the USSR. Inspection of the 5TH Infantry Division in the fall of 1941 in Tatishchevo.

Polish army in the East. Under the command of General W. Anders, these army units managed to leave the USSR in time and move to the Middle East. The army units consisted of two infantry divisions, a sapper brigade, an artillery group, a cavalry regiment, sapper and communications battalions, auxiliary services, and a reserve infantry division. They were organized into the 2ND Polish Corps.

blame on the Soviets. The Polish Government in Exile in London arranged for an inspection of the graves by the Swiss Red Cross, an impartial international organization. The Soviets, whose situation on the Eastern Front had markedly improved, used this as a pretext to break off relations with the Polish Government in Exile. The inspection by Red Cross doctors clearly demonstrated that the killings in 1940 were carried out on Stalin's order. More recently, this was confirmed by Gorbachev on the strength of the now declassified NKVD (secret police) documents. This explained the small number of officers reporting to Buzuluk to join the Polish army. In all, fifteen thousand officers were taken prisoner by the Soviets in 1939 and killed in the spring of 1940. Of those, 4,321 bodies were discovered by the Germans in Katyń in 1943. It is now known that the remaining officers were killed by the Soviets in Twer (called Kalinin during the Soviet rule) and in Kharkov in Ukraine.

ITALIAN CAMPAIGN AND THE BATTLE OF MONTE CASSINO

At the beginning of 1944, after moving from Iraq to Palestine, the 2ND Polish Corps moved to Egypt and then on to southern Italy. After a few smaller engagements in southern Italy, the Corps was moved to the vicinity of the Monte Cassino monastery. Because of its commanding location, the massif overlooked and controlled the Naples-Rome road and railway line. The Germans, realizing its strategic value, had fortified and connected it to their Gustav Line fortifications stretching across the Italian "boot" and manned it with the crack 1ST Parachute Division. Three attempts to take the monastery had

Polish army in the USSR. The bodies of 4,000 Polish officers murdered by the Soviets in 1940 in Katyń.

already been made by the Allies, but without success. The first attempt was made by the units of the American Fifth Army, an Algerian formation of the French Corps and units of the British Eighth Army. The following two attempts by the New Zealand Corps were also unsuccessful. On March 24, 1944, General Leese, commander of the British Eighth Army, asked General Anders if the 2ND Polish Corps would undertake a capturing of the monastery. He received an affirmative reply.

The attack, at 1:00 A.M. on May 12, 1944, was preceded by a two-hour, 800-gun artillery barrage along the entire front. Two Polish divisions advanced, ascending rocky 30 to 45-degree inclines and enduring the constant fire of well-positioned, fortified German artillery and machine guns. The fighting continued throughout the night and until the following afternoon. There was no chance of bringing reinforcements, as all paths and roads were covered by German fire. Yet, despite the enormous fire power, the Allied artillery did not succeed in silencing the German artillery; and, in the evening of May 12, General Anders gave the order to withdraw to the original departure points. The withdrawal ended on May 13. At 7:00 A.M. on May 17, fresh battalions of the two Polish divisions began the attack. This time, despite the terrain, Polish tanks were sent up the mountain. Those which broke down or were damaged by mines were pushed into the precipice to make room for those behind. Also, weighing two and a half tons each, anti-tank canons were disassembled below, dragged up the mountain piece by piece under the cover of darkness, reassembled and, at the time of the attack, opened up on the Germans at point-blank range.

In the late afternoon of May 17, the critical point was reached; it was impossible to gain any more ground. Exhausted soldiers laid hidden behind the rocks. The Germans were

Second Polish Corps in Italy. Battle for Monte Cassino. Polish infantry charging up the Phantom Hill using hand grenades.

Second Polish Corps in Italy. Tanks were brought into action during the battle for Monte Cassino. The Polish sign, translated into English, reads: "Don't be stupid, keep the distance, don't let them kill you."

Second Polish Corps in Italy. In the battle for Monte Cassino, the Poles partially disassembled anti-tank artillery pieces, hauled them to the vicinity of the German bunkers, and fired at the enemy at point-blank range.

equally as exhausted. Victory depended on the strength of will of each side. The 2ND Polish Corps did not have any reserves, but General Anders decided to throw everything he had into the final attack: bloodied battalions from the first engagement, commandos, drivers, and mechanics. On the morning of May 18, a renewed attack was launched; but, during the night, the crack German paratroopers had had enough and withdrew, leaving only a token defense behind. Thus, at 10:20 A.M. on May 18, 1944, a patrol of the 12TH Cavalry Regiment hoisted the Polish flag upon the ruins of the monastery. The road to Rome was open. On June 4, 1944, the American Fifth Army entered the Eternal City.

Not long afterwards, the 2ND Polish Corps fought a victorious eight-day battle for Loreto; moving north along the Adriatic, they captured Ancona, broke through the Gothic Line, and took Faenza. On April 21, 1945, the Italian Campaign ended with the 2ND Polish Corps' liberation of Bologna.

POLISH ARMED FORCES IN THE SOVIET UNION

There were many freed Polish Gulag prisoners who did not reach General Anders's army in time to join its evacuation to Iran and the Middle East in 1942. Those ex-prisoner of war soldiers left behind in the Soviet Union, together with conscripts incorporated into the army when the Soviets reached Polish territories, were formed sequentially into the 1ST, 2ND, and 3RD Polish armies. These armies fell under the command of a handful of Polish officers who agreed to cooperate with the Soviets. Unable to resurrect the fifteen thousand Polish officers

Second Polish Corps in Italy. Battle for Monte Cassino. A Polish bugler plays the bugle call in the Monastery ruins.

Second Polish Corps in Italy. Battle for Monte Cassino. At ten o'clock on May 18, 1944, a Polish flag flew over the ruins of the Monte Cassino Monastery. The road to Rome was open.

Second Polish Corps in Italy. On April 21, 1945, Polish tanks, greeted by cheering crowds, enter Bologna, Italy.

Second Polish Corps in Italy. Polish and American soldiers meet in the streets of Bologna on April 21, 1945.

they had murdered, the Soviets added Soviet Russian officers to the Polish Army who often could only speak a few words of Polish. The overall command was Soviet. The Soviets made token attempts to draw upon Polish military tradition, whenever it did not collide with their own interests. For example, the Polish army in the Soviet Union had military chaplains—something completely unheard of in the Soviet army.

From October 12 to 14, 1943, the First Polish Infantry Division made an assault on Lenino near Smolensk and sustained twenty-five percent losses. Later, the First Polish Army fought in central Poland and along the Baltic coast. The Second Polish Army fought in Czechoslovakia, and the 1ST Kosciuszko Infantry Division fought in Berlin around the Reich Chancellery and the Reichstag. At this stage of the war, the Polish role in the Soviet drive westward was fairly substantial, contributing 200,000 troops; this was approximately ten percent of the force taking part in Zhukov's and Koniev's drive on Berlin, not counting Polish auxiliary units located behind the front in Poland and eastern Germany.

NORMANDY, BELGIUM, HOLLAND AND WILHELMSHAVEN

The 1ST Polish Armored Division and the 1ST Polish Independent Parachute Brigade were organized in Britain from 1941–1943. A shortage of manpower presented the greatest problem. Recruits were brought in from the Middle East (ex-Gulag prisoners from the 2ND Polish Corps), the United States, and from other countries. Finally, in the late spring of 1944, both units were ready for action. General Stanisław Maczek was commander of the 1ST Armored Division which was scheduled to take part in the second stage of the Normandy invasion. The division landed in France between July 29 and August 4, 1944, and was assigned to the Second Canadian Corps.

On August 7, two months after the Allied invasion of Normandy, the German Seventh Army launched a counterattack in the direction of Avranches, with the hope of destroying the

Polish army formations under Soviet control. Advancing First Polish Division during the battle at Lenino.

Polish army formations under Soviet control. First Polish Army artillery units in action on the Byelorussian front.

Polish army formations under Soviet control. A column of Polish 2ND Howitzer Brigade passing the Brandenburg Gate in Berlin on May 8, 1945.

Allied armies which had broken out of beachhead. This 70,000-strong German force was at Mortain, while the Allied armies made converging sweeps to ensure that it did not emerge from the trap. Suddenly aware of their danger, the German forces tried to disengage and force a way back through the remaining outlets. On August 15, General Maczek's tanks crossed the Dives River and raced to cut the three German escape routes southeast of Falaise. The Poles captured the last gap at Chambois on August 19. An inferno of death and destruction followed, as the enemy tried to hammer a way through the sector

77

held by the Poles and the Allies launched salvo after salvo of shells on the German Seventh Army's men, guns, tanks and vehicles. Though other Allied units were approaching as fast as they could, the Poles were virtually isolated as the German 1ST and 12TH divisions, fighting with the desperation of the doomed, launched repeat attacks. As tank fought tank at close range and men engaged in hand-to-hand struggles, the Poles were running short of food and ammunition and their wounded could not be evacuated. Not until August 21 was the pressure relieved. H.D. Ziman, a British correspondent writing for *The Daily Telegraph* on that day, described the battle:

> The entire German force, with supporting infantry, bore down on the Poles, who were temporarily out of touch with their allies on either flank. The Poles stood their ground. Compelled to face about—for the enemy force had approached them from behind as well—and with both flanks exposed, they fought back all day against the Germans, who emerged in wave after wave from the cover provided by the forest of Gouffen. . . . Although some twenty thousand Germans had managed to slip out before the encirclement was completed by the arrival of American and Canadian troops, the drive, initiative and fighting quality of Maczek's men were responsible for one of the greatest disasters which the German army suffered in France.

After re-equipment, the 1ST Polish Armored Division took part in liberating northern France, Belgium and Holland. In Holland, the Division liberated Breda. General Maczek preferred to command his troops from the leading tank, and he

The 1ST Polish Armored Division on the Western Front. General S. Maczek (top left), the division commander, in a leading tank.

always sought to minimize damage to the towns which he liberated. He took Breda in a surprise attack from the east without firing a single shot into the town. Hence, he earned the undying gratitude of the inhabitants, who awarded honorary citizenship to the entire Polish division. On May 6, 1945, the division hoisted a Polish flag over Wilhelmshaven in Germany, the main German U-boat base. General Maczek was one of the officers who accepted the surrender of the German forces.

The 1ST Polish Armored Division on the Western Front. Tanks of the 10TH Mounted Rifle Regiment near Caen at the beginning of the Falaise operations.

The 1ST Polish Armored Division on the Western Front. Destruction suffered by the Germans during the Falaise battle.

The 1ˢᵀ Polish Armored Division on the Western Front. Van Slobbe, the mayor of Breda, Holland, giving a welcome speech to the 1ˢᵀ Division which liberated Breda.

The 1ˢᵀ Polish Armored Division on the Western Front. General S. Maczek being decorated with the Legion of Honor by the French chief of staff, General A.P. Juin.

The 1ˢᵀ Polish Armored Division on the Western Front. The Wilhelmshafen German commander surrenders this main German U-boat base to Colonel A. Grudzinski.

ARNHEM

The 1ST Polish Independent Parachute Brigade was formed in England and was originally intended for use in support of the Polish Underground during its uprising. Before the Warsaw Uprising, in the summer of 1944, the British felt that they would be unable to support the brigade once it was dropped into Poland and insisted that the brigade be used to support operations in western Europe. The Poles had little choice but to accept. It was decided that the parachute brigade would drop during Operation Market-Garden (Arnhem) in September 1944. Yet it should be mentioned that the Polish commander of the brigade, General Stanisław Sosabowski, was aghast when informed of the details of the British drop; he felt that Operation Market-Garden was too hastily planned and poorly conceived.

The plan called for the Polish brigade to be dropped on day D+2 to support the British 1ST Airborne Division which was assigned to capture the bridge over the Lower Rhine at Arnhem. The American 82ND and 101ST airborne divisions were dropped south of Nijmegen and north of Eindhoven. The Dutch Underground had not been informed of the drops, and therefore could not help by way of intelligence and support. The Polish brigade's drop was postponed for three days because of bad weather. Finally, in the late afternoon of September 21, the Polish brigade was dropped near the village of Driel, on the south side of the Lower Rhine—not on the side where the British 1ST Airborne was holding the bridgehead. The drop itself was a disaster. One battalion of the brigade was ordered back to England because of bad weather. There was no air cover for the Dakotas carrying the paratroopers, and twenty-five German *Messershmitt* fighters were blasting the defenseless transport planes out of the sky with complete impunity. To make matters worse, the Germans had tracked and timed the formations as they flew from Dunkirk, and now, with reinforcements, the area bristled with firing anti-aircraft guns. In the Oosterbeek perimeter of the British-held bridgehead 2.5 miles away, the drop caused a momentary halt in the battle: every German gun was now concentrated on the swaying Polish paratroopers. Though shocked by the savagery of the combined air and anti-aircraft fire, most of the Polish brigade miraculously made the drop zone. Even as they landed, flak and mortar shells fired from the German tanks burst among them. Disregarding the fire, Dutch Red Cross teams ran to help the wounded Poles.

According to the plan, the brigade was to cross the Rhine by ferry to get to the British; but, the ferry had been destroyed in the fighting. Therefore, the Poles attempted to cross the 400-yard river at night, under the cover of darkness, in four rubber dinghies on a hawser. Each dinghy could accommodate up to six men at a time. Under German fire, the Poles were slowly getting across, but were suffering heavy casualties. At 3:00 A.M. the operation was stopped. Only fifty men had been ferried across the river. At midnight on September 23, under heavy fire and suffering heavy casualties, some of the Polish paratroopers crossed the river in sixteen boats left over from the 82ND United States Division assault on the Waal River. Only 250 Poles made it to the northern bank, and 200 reached the beleaguered British 1ST Airborne Division at Arnhem. The Polish remnants withdrew together with the remnants of the British 1ST Airborne Division. The lost battle and heavy casualties were particularly hard on the survivors: they knew that the Warsaw Uprising, which had began on August 1, was dying and they could do nothing to help.

The Polish Airborne Brigade at Arnhem. Polish anti-tank artillery which landed on September 18, 1944.

The Polish Airborne Brigade at Arnhem. General S. Sosabowski (right), commander of the brigade during the operation near Driel.

The Polish Airborne Brigade at Arnhem. Polish paratroopers in firing positions on the southern bank of the Rhine.

THE WARSAW UPRISING:
AUGUST 1 – OCTOBER 5, 1944

On August 1, 1944, at 5:00 P.M., the 40,000-strong underground Home Army in Warsaw came out of hiding and attacked German positions, offices and patrols around the city. An uprising—an open struggle against the Germans at the conclusion of the armed underground resistance—had been the ultimate objective of the Home Army since its inception in Warsaw and before its fall during the last days of the 1939 campaign. Indeed, officers and men of the Home Army could not imagine ending the war without settling the score with the brutal and universally despised occupant. Had an order to start an uprising not been given, a series of spontaneous, uncoordinated actions against the Germans by individual Home Army units would have ensued with dire consequences for the insurgents. The uprising was to halt the implementation of German plans to convert Warsaw into a Stalingrad-like fortress, and also to prevent the Germans from killing or driving out inhabitants and razing the city to the ground. An uprising would demonstrate to the world the Polish resolve in fighting the Germans, particularly in Warsaw. It would also reassert Polish independence and the preexisting political authority of the legal Polish Government in London before the Soviet army had entered Warsaw. This was particularly important in view of Stalin's hostility towards independent Poland, as demonstrated by the hostile actions of the Soviets towards Home Army units helping Soviet troops against the Germans. On July 26, 1944, the Polish Government in Exile in London transmitted an authorization to its delegate in occupied Poland to decide the date and time of the start of the Warsaw Uprising. On the afternoon of July 31, 1944,

Colonel Monter, commander of the Home Army in the Warsaw district, notified General Bór, commander in chief of the Home Army, that Soviet tanks were approaching Warsaw on the eastern bank of the Vistula. General Bór issued an order for the uprising to begin at 5:00 P.M. on the following day, August 1, 1944.

On August 1, the Home Army had the following weapons at its disposal: one thousand carbines, three hundred submachine guns, sixty light machine guns, seven heavy machine guns, thirty-five special carbines and bazookas, seventeen hundred revolvers, and twenty-five thousand hand grenades. Some weapons were produced in secret shops by the insurgents themselves, prior to and during the uprising. The most common were "Lightning" submachine guns of Polish design, and "Filipinka" and "Sidolówka" hand grenades. Gasoline-filled bottles were used as anti-tank weapons. Ammunition was very scarce; there were one hundred ninety rounds per carbine, five hundred rounds per light machine gun, and three hundred rounds per submachine gun. The main source of additional weapons and ammunition would be the enemy.

Who were the insurgents, the Home Army underground soldiers who, for five years of German occupation, had been preparing themselves for the uprising? They came from all social strata: the rich and poor, university professors, teachers, high school and university students, artists, unskilled laborers and so on.

For the first two days, the insurgents attacked German positions around the town, but were not sufficiently well-armed to take them all. By the fifth day of the uprising, the Germans organized themselves and proceeded methodically, from block to block, annihilating insurgents, civilians (the Germans generally did not take prisoners), and destroying buildings. They

The Warsaw Uprising. The Home Army Battalion "Pięść" ("Fist"), before going into action.

The Warsaw Uprising. Young boys, armed only with gasoline-filled bottles serving as anti-tank weapons, on the way to barricades.

The Warsaw Uprising. The Polish insurgents did not have the luxury of a plentiful supply of ammunition—theirs was to be used sparingly. The poster reads: "ONE BULLET, ONE GERMAN," a warning not to waste ammunition.

were not always successful. Captain "Lech" Zagórski, commander of a Polish sector on Grzybowska Street, described the action in his area on Tuesday, August 15:

At five o'clock this morning, the Germans threw in everything they had. Wave after wave of Junkers and Stuka dive bombers flew over, and Tiger and Panther tanks moved towards us along the surrounding streets. The din of bombs and shrapnel, the roar of engines, the thunder of tons of metal crashing down, all mingled with the rumble of falling walls and roofs, the rattle of machine guns and the shriek of bullets overhead, like a storm gone mad. Begrimed runners hurried along in the shelter of walls with messages from officers on the barricades. They all told what they had seen. On one street, tanks smashed through one of our barricades. Then, Captain Proboszcz appeared as though he'd risen out of the ground; he hurled a grenade at a tank and, immediately after the explosion, he leaped onto the tank, wrenched open the lid and shot the German driver at point-blank range from his revolver. Then, he grabbed the German's gun and hurried on. . . . The tanks on Rynkowa and Ciepła streets were moving along behind a crowd of civilians, who were being driven ahead to provide cover for the Germans. I gave the order to fire. Some of the civilians were hit and were left lying on the pavement. . . . Then, Major Zagończyk asked for me: 'I know you are in trouble; I'll do what I can to help with ammunition. But you have got to hold your street. You have got to. Can you do it?' I replied: 'We will hold out sir.' I started along the street. The smoke had died down a little. To my left was a deserted barricade; immediately below the corner block of apartments, the shell of a tank half-buried in a trench was smoldering. The firing had died down. I crossed the street and cautiously went up the barricade. I looked over the top and saw a powerful Tiger tank snarling halfway down Ciepła Street. But, I could hardly believe my eyes. It was retreating. Another tank stood near Krochmalna Street motionless. Its tracks had been ripped off. And near the barracks I saw a third tank dead with its cover open. . . . From across the battlefield two men appeared, clumsily scrambling past the smoldering tank. I hardly recognized Tadeusz and Puchacz, for they looked as if they'd dug themselves out of a heap of cement. Somehow they'd survived, hidden by the heavy balustrade of a balcony on the first floor immediately above the barricade. They'd let the tank come up to the barricade so they could not miss; for, although they were half-buried in rubble, their arms were free. . . . I reported back to Major Zagończyk by telephone: 'We have held our street. The Germans are retreating. We ought to send patrols out after them and try to man the barricades again. We ought to bring the wounded and bury the dead. But there are only six of us left. We have not a single bullet or grenade.'

SS formations deployed by the Germans against the insurgents were composed of common criminals (SS Brigade Dierlewanger and SS Storm Brigade RONA) who raped and killed without any regard to age or gender. On August 5, both units

The Warsaw Uprising. Courier (runner) girls maintained communication between various insurgent units. These girls, because of their bravery, commanded great respect among the insurgents.

The Warsaw Uprising. A courier girl poses for a photograph in front of a destroyed German tank.

launched an attack on the Wola sector. They went into battle with gusto, and by August 6 they had murdered more than forty thousand civilians, including women, children, hospital staff, priests, the wounded and the sick in the Wola and Ochota sectors.

The fiercest struggle took place in the defense of the Old Town, where the concentration of bombardment (the Germans used rail-mounted howitzers) was the highest encountered in World War II. Polish casualties were high, as were the German's. German losses exceeded fifty percent. German sources report that, on average, German casualties in the 33-day battle for Old Town amounted to one hundred fifty soldiers per day; insurgent casualties reached seventy-seven percent. Fifteen hundred armed insurgents, some lightly wounded, were evacuated to the city center through the sewers. Two hundred perished during the evacuation. Nearly twenty-five hundred of the gravely wounded who could not be evacuated were left behind in field hospitals, with hospital staff who, although facing certain death, chose to stay with their patients until the end. The commander of the Old Town sector, Colonel Wachnowski, also refused evacuation; only a direct order from Home Army commander General Bór compelled him to join his withdrawing soldiers. The ferocity of the fighting in the uprising, according to those Germans who also experienced Stalingrad, was far greater in Warsaw than that encountered in the Russian city.

There were air sorties from the west to drop essential supplies to the insurgents. But the Russians refused to grant landing rights for planes to refuel at Soviet bases. The air drops were not very effective, although they demanded great skill and heroism from the pilots. Only once, under the pressure of Western public opinion, did the Russians agree to allow the Allied planes to land on Soviet soil, on the airfield of Poltava in

The Warsaw Uprising. German prisoners captured after the Poles took the Telephone Exchange. The Poles (unlike the Germans) followed the Geneva convention in the treatment of German prisoners.

The Warsaw Uprising. Deliveries of the insurgents' press and general mail was taken over by the boy scouts.

The Warsaw Uprising. These soldiers came through sewers from the Old Town to the city center. Note their soldierly bearing even after several hours of passage in a fetid morass, in complete darkness and silence. (At any sound of movement down below, Germans tossed hand grenades through sewer manholes.)

Ukraine. On September 18, 110 United States air force B-17s participated in the mission in which two planes were lost. Captain "Lech" Zagórski remembered the drop:

> I had just got back to my quarters at Pańska Street and was listening to Wiślański's report when the sentry at the gate gave warning of aircraft approaching. I went out to look. There, straight ahead to the north and very high up, I saw aircraft coming over. They looked like silver birds in a blue sky. I counted twelve of them, then more and more until I lost count. The roar of their engines grew, for they were coming straight towards us. Someone was counting them aloud: '102, 105, 108. . . .' I looked through my binoculars. They were neither German nor Soviet. Then someone shouted: 'They are Liberators! And they are ours!' (In reality, they were Flying Fortresses and not Liberators, but for the insurgents the difference at that moment was immaterial.) Everyone ran out into the street and scrambled up into the rubble to get a better look. Then, dozens of small clouds appeared round the aircraft as the German AA opened fire. But they were out of range and the shells burst too low. Shrapnel began falling around us and I shouted to everyone to take cover, but nobody heeded. Then, three black dots fell away from the leading planes, to be followed at once by more and more, while little colored circles appeared over the dots—parachutes opening up. 'Parachutists!' Everyone went mad. They jumped up and down waving, hugging one another. . . . 'No, not parachutists—it's arms! They are dropping arms!' Now we could see the long metal containers more clearly, and

The Warsaw Uprising. The insurgents watch air drops from the American super-fortresses on September 18, 1944.

the first fell directly in our sector. Suddenly, there was a roar from the German positions: rifles, machine guns, grenades, mortars, artillery, the lot! They were firing at us along the whole length of their line. With Ryś and Genek I ran out to the first container which had fallen fortunately in a deep hollow. The metal fasteners opened easily, and inside we found boxes fitted with straps, ready to be slung over the shoulders. They contained British machine guns with ammo, and a few minutes later they were ready for firing. The men brought in more containers, and company commanders started to report to me by telephone how many they had obtained. At the same time, they all told me they were going out in full force against fierce German attack. I asked if they needed any reinforcements, but no one did. Each officer said that today their men would go out against the devil himself. Then, we opened the other containers; they contained Sten guns and ammo, equipment for sappers, mines, anti-tank weapons, medical supplies, and food, including corned beef, chocolate and crackers. The hands of the ambulance girls trembled a little as we handed over phials of blood for transfusions; the phials bore labels in Polish, for the blood had been donated by Poles at the Polish hospital in Edinburgh.

The struggle went on for sixty-three days. On September 29, the sixtieth day of the uprising, there was only food left for three more days. Repeated offers from the Polish Home Army to cooperate with the Soviet army remained unanswered. Towards the end of the uprising, Soviet aircraft dropped some supplies for the insurgents, but it was a token gesture: the drops were executed without parachutes and the weapons were so damaged by the impact that, in most cases, they were unusable. When the Home Army finally was forced to surrender, the Germans agreed to extend combatant status to the insurgents—meaning that the insurgents were to be treated as prisoners of war in accordance with the Geneva convention. By and large, this was adhered to by the Germans. Throughout the uprising, the Poles' treatment of German prisoners, including the wounded, was in conformance with the Geneva convention. The Warsaw civilians—those who had not been murdered or had not managed to escape—were sent to labor camps in Germany.

The combatants' strength was nearly equal at forty thousand men on each side, though in equipment and armaments the Germans had devastating superiority. The Germans lost 26,000 men in the fighting, the insurgents 22,200 men. A quarter of a million Polish civilians were murdered or killed. German materiel losses comprised 310 tanks, armored cars and self-propelled artillery (including 22 75-millimeter artillery pieces), and 340 trucks and cars. After the fighting, those civilians who had not been taken to labor camps were driven out of the city; and, at the personal order of Hitler, who decreed that Warsaw be erased from the maps, special German army units equipped with flamethrowers were brought in to destroy those houses which were still left standing after the fighting. Ninety percent of the city was destroyed. Although it would have been cheaper and easier to rebuild the city somewhere else, the Poles were determined to rebuild it in exactly the same spot where it had been before. To replicate and revive its pre-war charm and architectural beauty, reconstruction of the Old Town was painstakingly modeled after old paintings, sketches and photographs which had survived the war.

The Warsaw Uprising. Destruction of Warsaw during the uprising.

The Warsaw Uprising. Destruction of Warsaw during the uprising.

The following statistics illustrate the degree of Warsaw's depopulation and the subsequent restoration effort: before the war, Warsaw had 1.2 million inhabitants; from the beginning of October 1944, when the uprising ended and the entire population was driven out of the city by the Germans, until January 1945, when the Soviets finally came, the city had zero inhabitants; today, the population of Warsaw has reached 1.6 million.

But what became of the Soviet army, which was only a few miles away from Warsaw when the uprsing began on August 1, 1944? It halted its advance. The Polish 1ST Division units (from the Polish army formed in the Soviet Union), on their own initiative, established a bridgehead in Warsaw on the western side of the Vistula to help the insurgents. The Division held it for eight days, sustaining 5,600 casualties, without any help from other Soviet units in the area. Not until January 1945, long after the uprising had been suppressed, did the Soviets finally move, and by then they were merely "liberating" uninhabited ruins. It is now certain that Stalin, who forcibly introduced communism to Poland after the war, wanted to eliminate Polish patriots who opposed his communization plans. Ultimately, the Germans killed and murdered for him many of those patriots in Warsaw.

In eastern and central Poland, the Soviet army was glad to accept help from the Polish Home Army partisan units operating against the Germans. The cooperation most often ended once the Germans were defeated and the Poles were no longer needed in the area. The usual Soviet tactic was to invite a Polish commander and all officers to the Soviet headquarters, ostensibly for "consultation"; once there, the Soviets disarmed them, surrounding and disarming Polish partisans who were left without officers. The officers and those partisans who refused to join the Soviet army or its Polish counterpart were sent to

Post-war Poland. The Warsaw Old Town, leveled by the Germans during and after the uprising, was painstakingly rebuilt after the war by the Poles, using old paintings, sketches and photographs.

Gulags. This tactic was quickly noticed by Polish Home Army partisans, and they responded by continuing to operate against the Germans on their own and by not cooperating with the Soviets. Ultimately, the Soviet treacherous tactic contributed to the beginning of the anticommunist partisan movement which existed in Poland long after the defeat of Germany.

Post-war Poland. Tomb of the Unknown Soldier in Warsaw—a memento from Warsaw's destruction in the uprising.

EPILOGUE

On June 6, 1946, a Victory Parade was held in London. At the request of the Soviet government, Poles were not invited to take part. Thus Poland, which had been the first to say "NO" to Hitler and was the first to fight, was at Stalin's request excluded from the Victory celebrations. This was symptomatic of the treatment meted out to Poland by the Soviets and the Western Allies at Teheran, Yalta and Potsdam.

Poland fought against Hitler, together with the Allies on all European fronts—by land, sea, and air—from the very beginning until Germany was defeated. Poland won the war but lost the peace because Roosevelt and Churchill chose to appease Stalin at Teheran and Yalta. Was the Polish war effort adequate, considering Poland's capabilities? Was the effort of the Western leaders who negotiated with Stalin adequate, considering their advantage of nuclear monopoly from 1945 until 1949? That advantage was squandered in the European theater, and nearly 100 million people from eastern and central Europe were abandoned to the Soviets.

After forty-four years of communist domination, Poland finally achieved freedom and sovereignty. Poland's Solidarity movement led the way, creating a vortex of ideas and events which pulled in the neighboring countries and eventually led to the collapse of the Soviet Union.

BIBLIOGRAPHY

IN ENGLISH:

Baluk, Stefan Starba. *Poles on the Fronts of World War II.* Warsaw: Books International, 1995.

Davies, Norman. *God's Playground.* New York: Columbia University Press, 1982.

Garlinski, Jozef. *Poland in the Second World War.* New York: Hippocrene Books, 1985.

——. *The Enigma War.* New York: Charles Scribner's Sons, 1980.

Karski, Jan. *The Great Powers and Poland 1919–1945: From Versailles to Yalta.* Lanham, MD: University Press of America, Inc., 1995.

Kurek, Ewa. *Your Life is Worth Mine.* New York: Hippocrene Books, 1997.

Lukas, Richard C. *Forgotten Holocaust: The Poles Under German Occupation, 1939–1945.* New York: Hippocrene Books, 1997.

Ryan, Cornelius. *A Bridge Too Far.* Popular Library Edition. Copyright 1974 by Cornelius Ryan.

Watt, Richard M. *Bitter Glory.* New York: Simon & Schuster, 1982.

Zagórski, Waclaw. *Seventy Days.* London: Panther Books, 1959.

Zaloga, Steven J. *The Polish Army: 1939–1945.* London: Osprey Publishing, 1982.

Zamoyski, Adam. *The Forgotten Few.* New York: Hippocrene Books, 1995.

——. *The Polish Way.* New York: Hippocrene Books, 1993.

Zawodny, J. K. *Nothing But Honour*. Stanford, CA: Hoover Institution Press, 1978.

The German New Order in Poland. Published for the Polish Ministry of Information by Hutchinson & Co. Publishers, Ltd., London, circa 1942.

IN POLISH:

Gruzewski, Jan, & Stanislaw Kopf. *Dni Powstania-Kronika Fotograficzna Walczącej Warszawy*. Warszawa: PAX, 1957.

Jurga, Tadeusz. *Obrona Polski 1939*. Warszawa: Instytut Wydawniczy PAX, 1990.

Kołodziejski et al. *Kronika Dziejow Polski*. Krakow: Copyright Wydawnictwo Ryszard Kluszczynski, 1995.

Kopf, Stanislaw. *Lata Okupacji*. Warszawa: Copyright Stanislaw Kopf, 1989.

Korboński, Stefan. *Polskie Państwo Podziemne*. Philadelphia: Promyk, 1983.

Kosiarz, Edmund. *Flota Orla Bialego*. Gdansk: Wydawnictwo Morskie, 1984.

Krzyżakowa et al. *Warszawa 1945–1970*. Warszawa: Sport i Turystyka, 1970.

Strzembosz, Tomasz. *Akcje Zbrojne Podziemnej Warszawy 1939–1944*. Warszawa: Państwowy Instytut Wydawniczy, 1978.

Szmagier, Krzysztof. *General Anders i Jego Żolnierze*. Warszawa: Instytut Wydawniczy PAX, 1993.

Wańkowicz, Melchior. *Bitwa o Monte Cassino*. Rzym-Mediolan: Wydawnictwo Oddziału Kultury i Prasy Drugiego Polskiego Korpusu, 1945.

Wielecki, Henryk. *Pod Znakiem Srebrnego i Zlotego Orla*. Warszawa: Muzeum Wojska Polskiego, 1998.

Wojewódzki, Michal. *Akcja V-1, V-2*. Warszawa: Instytut Wydawniczy PAX, 1975.

Wysznacki, Leszek, ed. *Stolica*. No. 1153. Warszawa: 1970.

Zielinski, Józef. *Asy Polskiego Lotnictwa*. Warszawa: Agencja Lotnicza Altair, 1995.

INDEX

Other Illustrated History titles from Hippocrene Books . . .

THE CELTIC WORLD: AN ILLUSTRATED HISTORY
Patrick Lavin

From the valleys of Bronze Age Urnfielders to the works of 20TH century Irish-American literary greats Mary Higgins Clark and Seamus Heaney, Patrick Lavin leads the reader on an entertaining and informative journey through 182 captivating pages of Celtic history, culture, and tradition, including 50 illustrations and maps. This concise yet insightful survey of Celtic history is a handy reference guide for a variety of readers—young scholars, travelers, and those simply interested in Celtic heritage.

Patrick Lavin was born in County Roscommon, Ireland. He is a graduate of California State University (Northridge), and is retired from service with the United States Government. An avid history enthusiast, he spends his retirement years researching Celtic and Irish history and writing nonfiction books and articles. His works include *Thank You Ireland* (co-author) and *Celtic Ireland: Roots and Routes*. He currently resides in Tucson, Arizona.

185 pages • 5 x 7 • 50 b/w illustrations/maps
• $14.95hc • 0-7818-0731-X • W • (582)

IRELAND: AN ILLUSTRATED HISTORY

Henry Weisser

Erin go bragh! While it is easy to appreciate the natural beauty of Ireland, the Emerald Isle's history is also a rich and complex subject of study. Spanning prehistoric and Celtic Ireland to modern times, this concise, illustrated volume examines the people, religion, social changes, and politics that have evolved into the tradition of modern Ireland. Henry Weisser takes the reader on a journey through Ireland's past—to show how historic events have left an indelible mark on everything from architecture and economy, to the spirit and lifestyles of the Irish people.

Henry Weisser received his Ph.D. from Columbia University and is Professor of History at Colorado State University. He has taught Irish history for many years, and has led groups of students and teachers on trips to Ireland. He is the author of seven books, including *Hippocrene Companion Guide to Ireland*, *Companion Guide to Britain*, and *USA Guide to the Rocky Mountain States*.

166 pages • 5 x 7 • 50 b/w illustrations/maps • $11.95hc • 0-7818-0693-3 • W • (782)

ISRAEL: AN ILLUSTRATED HISTORY

David C. Gross

Despite its physical size, Israel from earliest times to the present has always been a major player on the world stage. The birthplace of Judaism, which in turn became the mother religion of Christianity and Islam, Israel holds a very special place in the minds and hearts of hundreds of millions of people, particularly in the Western world. This concise, illustrated volume offers the reader an informative, panoramic view of this remarkable land, from biblical days to the 21ST century. Since its foundation a scant 50 years ago, Israel has emerged as a veritable magnet and spiritual resource for Jews and Gentiles alike. With topics exploring art, literature, sculpture, music, science, politics, religion and more, here is a wonderful gift book for travelers, students, or anyone seeking to expand their knowledge of Israeli history, culture, and heritage.

David C. Gross, author/editor of 21 published books in the field of Judaica, has visited Israel some 35 times—as a journalist, editor, translator and publisher. The prime ministers he has interviewed over the years include Ben-Gurion, Eshkol, Meir, Rabin, and Shamir. He studied at Brooklyn College and at the Herzliah Teachers Seminary.

160 pages • 5 x 7 • 50 b/w photos/illustrations
• $11.95hc • 0-7818-0756-5 • W • (24)

MEXICO: AN ILLUSTRATED HISTORY
Michael Burke

This handy historical guide traces Mexico from the peasant days of the Olmecs to the late 20TH century. With over 150 pages and 50 illustrations, the reader discovers how events of Mexico's past have left an indelible mark on the politics, economy, culture, spirit, and growth of this country and its people. Michael Burke's own extensive experience and research in Mexico allows him to explore in depth the issues of social class and power, dependency and conquest, and the fortitude of this remarkable country.

Michael Burke is Professor of History at Villanova University. He is author of *Hippocrene Companion Guide to Mexico*.

183 pages • 5 x 7 • 50 b/w illustrations • $11.95hc • 0-7818-0690-9 • W • (585)

RUSSIA: AN ILLUSTRATED HISTORY

Joel Carmichael

Encompassing one-sixth of the earth's land surface—the equivalent of the whole North American continent—Russia is the largest country in the world. Renowned historian Joel Carmichael presents Russia's rich and expansive past—upheaval, reform, social change, growth—in an easily accessible and concentrated volume. From the Tatar's reign to modern-day Russia, the book spans seven centuries of cultural, social and political events.

This is a book to be enjoyed by a diverse audience; from young scholars to those interested in Russian history, here is the perfect gift idea, a handy guide for travelers, and a wonderfully concise yet extensive survey of Russian history.

Joel Carmichael is a graduate of Columbia University, Oxford University and the Sorbonne. He has written many books on Russian history, including *A Cultural History of*

Russia, A Short History of the Russian Revolution, Trotsky, and *Stalin's Masterpiece.*

252 pages • 5 x 7 • 50 b/w illustrations
• $14.95hc • 0-7818-0689-5 • W • (781)